Performance Management *Revisited*

A toolkit for all those involved in the performance
management of headteachers, teachers and support staff

Michele Robbins

Adamson Publishing

© Michele Robbins 2007

Published by Adamson Publishing Ltd
8 The Moorings, Norwich, NR3 3AX
tel: 01603 623336 fax: 01603 624767
e-mail: info@adamsonbooks.com
www.adamsonbooks.com

ISBN 9780-948543-52-4

British Library Cataloguing in Publication Data:
A catalogue record for this book is available from the British Library

Design by Geoff Shirley

Printed and bound by Impress Print, Corby

Contents

Acknowledgements

I am very grateful for the considerable support I received from colleagues in schools who have generously shared their documentation with me. In particular I would like to thank Banbury School in Oxfordshire, Collingwood College in Surrey, Edgbarrow School in Bracknell Forest and Uxbridge Technology College in Hillingdon. I have taken the liberty to modify some aspects of those documents that I have used to take account of the fact that the toolkit is for all phases. I have in several cases combined different proformas, removing references to school-specific supporting materials noted in the original source material. I have also created new material based on my experience as a performance management consultant and external adviser.

I hope that the result will be practical working models to support the implementation of the policy.

Introduction

The toolkit is intended to be used as a flexible resource to support all those involved in the implementation of performance management in schools. This includes headteachers, school improvement partners (SIPs), teachers, support staff and governors. It is important to note that the Regulations do not apply to:

- teachers in their induction year
- teachers undergoing capability procedures
- teachers on contracts of less than one term.

The twin and closely related aims of the strategy are to continue to drive up standards in schools and to motivate and develop staff. A well-run scheme will be regarded by staff as an entitlement, not a burden. If it is effective it will ensure that:

- all staff are aware of the vision, aims and objectives of the school
- each individual understands what s/he has to do to help to achieve those objectives
- each individual has the skills, knowledge and information necessary to do what has been agreed.

These principles underpin the approach adopted throughout the toolkit. Successful implementation requires that the Self-Evaluation Form (SEF), school improvement plan, job descriptions and the continuing professional development strategy underpin the process.

Although the national strategy and policy on performance management apply only to teaching staff, consideration of the principles noted above raises a significant question about the wisdom of omitting support staff. Many schools recognise the important role they play, and include them in the process, even though that is not yet a statutory requirement. Therefore, this toolkit includes guidance and proformas to support application of the policy to support staff.

The toolkit is organised as follows:

- a brief overview of the context, highlighting the main differences in approach effective from 1 September 2007
- guidance on developing the policy
- an overview of the cycle, noting the way it has changed from the previous model
- further information about each stage of the cycle
- proformas to support implementation of the cycle with headteachers, teachers and support staff.

The proformas in this book may help you to adapt existing material or even create new material. Having customised them, it is recommended that you create electronic versions for ease of circulation and use.

Context

Performance management or appraisal has been in existence in schools for 20 years. It was brought into focus in 2000 when resources were made available to schools to buy in consultants to train all staff. Subsequently, in 2003 the guidance was revised and re-launched. Regulations introduced in 2006 refine and update the earlier Regulations to bring them into line with the 2002 Education Act.

A number of other national strategies are highly pertinent to the performance management process. These include:

- the **National Agreement** on workforce remodelling in which teachers/headteachers working with qualified support staff have conditions of service that enable them to focus on their core roles of teaching and learning. Integral to this is the need to protect work-life balance. Mindful of this, meetings should not happen during lunchtimes and PPA time.

- The introduction of the **new pay system** which replaced management allowances with Teaching and Learning Responsibility allowances. Despite the fact that job descriptions will have been revised in that review process it is important to check them as part of the annual performance management cycle.

- The introduction of the **SEF** to support whole school self-evaluation and strategic planning. Self-evaluation processes will help to generate evidence to underpin the monitoring of progress with objectives. The priorities for development, taken forward to the school improvement plan, will underpin objective-setting. Monitoring of progress with objectives will generate evidence for the SEF. These key processes must be consistent and coherent.

- The Children Act and the five **Every Child Matters Outcomes**. These feature large in many schools' improvement plans and policies and so will influence objectives.

- The need to distribute leadership and **plan for succession in schools**. This will be an issue when deciding reviewers. Fulfilling the role presents a career development opportunity.

- **Developing People to Support Learning, a skills strategy for the wider workforce**. This aims to help schools to develop new ways of training and deploying their support staff, supported by a framework of standards and qualifications and extended training opportunities.

The Training and Development Agency (TDA), together with the Rewards and Incentives Group (RIG), has been responsible for rolling out the performance management strategy, including providing training and resources for all those involved. A range of resources can be found on the TDA website:

http://www.tda.gov.uk/teachers/performance_management.aspx.

The resources include a comprehensive briefing sheet on frequently asked questions.

The policy and process

As in the earlier roll-outs, a model policy (*Model Performance Management for Schools*, on the TDA website) has been circulated which schools are strongly advised to adopt. It has been agreed by all the major unions except the NUT. In each school it is important to consult with all staff and union representatives when establishing and revising the policy.

In the model policy those aspects required by regulation are noted in bold, while it also presents various options on quality assurance, objective-setting, and governor reviewers to be decided on at the discretion of the governing body after full consultation with the headteacher and staff. These are given below, as in the model policy.

Quality assurance

• Moderation by the headteacher

(a)The headteacher may be the reviewer for all teachers.

Comment.

This would work in a small school but has the disadvantage that it would not help to develop leadership skills in other staff. In any case, the governing body will need to decide the optimum number of staff for each reviewer to work with, bearing in mind their other responsibilities and the need to ensure the process is given due time and attention.

(b) The headteacher may delegate the reviewer role to the line managers of teachers for whom s/he is not the line manager him/herself. In these circumstances the headteacher may decide to moderate all the **planning statements (not the review statements) to check that plans recorded in the statements of teachers at the school are consistent between those who have similar experience and similar levels of responsibility and that they comply with the school's performance management policy, the Regulations and the requirements of equality legislation.**

(c) Having delegated the reviewer role, the headteacher may decide to moderate a sample of planning statements to check **that the plans recorded in the statements of teachers at the school are consistent between those who have similar experience and similar levels of responsibility and that they comply with the school's performance management policy, the Regulations and the requirements of equality legislation.**

(d) Having delegated the reviewer role the headteacher may decide not to moderate at all.

Comment

Given that the system has been in place for several years it is likely that many reviewers are highly experienced so the headteacher may decide to focus on checking the work of new reviewers or may perhaps decide to sample each reviewer's work. Alternatively they may decide not to moderate at all.

• Quality assurance by the governing body

The process here is different to that described above in that the governing body doesn't have different planning statements to compare and contrast. So its options are:

(a) Nominate the chair of the governing body, who will not be involved in the headteacher's performance management or any appeal regarding the headteacher's performance management, to **ensure that the headteacher's planning statement is consistent with the school's improvement priorities and complies with the school's performance management policy and the Regulations.**

Comment

This is matter for judgement. Many governing bodies prefer to have the chair involved in the planning, monitoring and reviewing process. However, if there is any likelihood of an appeal, it may be better to keep the chair in reserve.

(b) The governing body may nominate one, two or three governors who will not be involved in the headteacher's performance management or any appeal regarding the headteacher's performance management to ensure that the headteacher's planning statement is consistent with the school's improvement priorities and complies with the school's performance management policy and the Regulations.

Comment

If this option is chosen the governing body needs to be mindful of the number of governors who will be involved in the overall process. See "Identifying and Training Reviewers" on page 13.

(c) The governing body may choose not to quality assure the planning statement.

Comment

In the earlier model governing bodies had the support of trained external advisers. That role has now been assumed by the school improvement partners, who may or may not have been trained for that aspect of the role. That's one factor to consider. Another is the level of experience of the governor reviewers.

Objective-setting

The options here are:

(a) All teachers including the headteacher, will have no more than .... objectives.

(b) Teachers, including the headteachers, will not necessarily have the same number of objectives.

Comment

The number actually decided may be dependent on the scope. It is important to remember that there should be sufficient number to gain a clear perspective on how each individual is approaching his/her work without trying to cover all the major responsibilities held.

(c) All teachers will have a whole school objective.

(d) All teachers, including the headteacher, will have a team objective, as appropriate.

Comment

This would not mean that the actions and performance criteria will be uniform. For example, there may be a whole-school objective to improve behaviour for learning. How that is interpreted for each teacher will be dependent on the performance of the learners for whom they have responsibility and the strengths and areas for development of their own professional practice.

Appointment of governor reviewers

The governing body has the following options:

(a) It may appoint two or three governors.

Comment

The word "may" only applies to the choice between two or three.

(b) For schools with a religious character at least one of the two or three must be a foundation governor.

(c) In VA schools if two governors are identified at least one must be a foundation governor. If three governors are involved not less than two must be foundation governors.

Comment

The decision about which governors should be involved should be made by the governing body. Governors will need to consider the skills and attributes that will lead to the process being fair, objective and rigorous.

The headteacher has the right to request that a governor reviewer is replaced if s/he believes the governor to be unsuitable for professional reasons.

School improvement partners (SIPs)

Once the local authority has appointed the SIP, that person will advise the governing body on the process. If no SIP has been appointed the governing body can appoint an external adviser. The governing body should negotiate with the SIP about their role in the process. It is appropriate to request that the SIP drafts the planning statement and objectives following the planning meeting. You may also ask that they provide advance advice in the same way that the external advisers did.

Appointment of reviewers for teachers

Where the headteacher is not the line manager for every teacher the headteacher will be the reviewer for those teachers s/he directly line manages and may delegate the role of reviewer in its entirety to the relevant line managers for some or all other teachers. In this case there is a further choice between reviewers reviewing all the teachers they line manage or fixing a maximum number. As noted earlier, it is important to take into account the overall responsibilities of the reviewers since, done thoroughly, implementing the cycle is quite a time-consuming process.

The headteacher decides on the delegation of reviewer duties and, as with the headteacher, teachers can request that a reviewer is replaced for professional reasons.

If the headteacher wishes to influence the decision regarding a pay award, s/he would have to act as the reviewer.

Appointment of reviewers for support staff

It may be the case that teachers line manage and performance manage support staff but many schools distribute leadership and give these roles to bursars, HLTAs and others. As with the reviewers of teaching staff they need training to carry out the role, a clear framework to operate within, and designated time to conduct meetings.

Timescale

The governing body can decide start and end times for the annual cycle, bearing in mind that the planning stage must be completed for all teachers by 31 October each year and for headteachers by 31 December.

The timing of the cycle will be influenced by the availability of performance data. In order to make sound judgements about success in relation to pupil progress objectives, it is important to have comparative data to draw upon. Similar robust data should underpin the target-setting process.

Given that the policy has to be reviewed annually, the effectiveness of the options selected will be reviewed and may lead to changes being made.

Classroom observation protocol

A further option is presented here concerning "drop-in" observations. The policy needs to state whether these will only be undertaken by the headteacher or whether the headteacher and other appropriate and designated staff will carry them out. Whichever option is chosen the evidence gathered will only be used where a revision to the performance management planning statement is deemed to be necessary.

Key aspects of the cycle

Planning

- Objectives set
- Classroom observation and evidence collection agreed
- Performance criteria for the above set
- Support, training and development agreed
- Timescales set

Monitoring & Supporting

- Monitoring of performance throughout the cycle
- Provision of agreed support
- Evidence collection
- Ongoing professional dialogue

Reviewing

- Overall assessment of individual's progress against the performance criteria
- Recommendations for pay progression made for eligible teachers
- No surprises

The main differences between the new model and earlier models are outlined on the next page. However many of those "differences" are simply re-stating what should have been in place in the previous model – for example, performance/success criteria being agreed at the outset and continuing professional development being an integral feature.

10

Performance Management Revisited

Differences from the previous system

Process and timeline

Previous position	Revised Regulations
No clear timeline.	Timeline for production of planning and review statement **See annex A for timeline.** Clarity on access to and retention of statements.
No date for the completion of the cycle leading to discontinuity between performance management and pay decisions.	The annual cycle must be completed by 31 October each year in time for pay recommendations to be made to the governing body (31 December for headteachers).
The Regulations excluded major elements of the process making them optional for schools, which led to inconsistencies. No provisions to limit any aspect of the process or have regard to work-life balance.	The Regulations governing the process are clearer and more detailed. Provisions in the Regulations to seek to limit workload arising from performance management.
Appeal: the teacher/headteacher could ask for a review of the outcomes, if there was disagreement about whether objectives had been met.	Clear right of appeal. The reviewee can appeal against any entry in his/her planning and review statement.

The planning meeting and CPD

At the planning meeting: no requirement to do anything but set objectives, leaving teachers unclear about expectations and the potential for other issues to be raised during the cycle and at the review.	At the planning meeting at the start of the cycle **objectives, classroom observation** and its focus, any **other evidence, support/development** to be provided, **timescales** and **performance criteria** against which progress will be judged at the end of the cycle must all be discussed and recorded reflecting any **pay progression criteria** for eligible teachers/headteachers. Objectives should, if they are achieved, contribute to improving pupil progress in the school. There is no stipulation about the number of objectives and no reference to leadership and management objectives or professional practice objectives, as in the previous model. The performance criteria must be determined as part of the planning meeting. This means that it must be clear at the outset how performance will be judged. It could be numerical – for example, $x\%$ of children reaching a specific level in a particular subject. If the objective is about something less tangible, e.g. improved self-esteem of learners, or greater independence as learners, the reviewee and reviewer will need to agree exactly what that will look like. What will children be doing that they are not doing now? What will the reviewee be doing to make that happen? The teacher/headteacher/support staff member must know at the outset what is expected of them.

Professional development considered when setting objectives.	Support, training and development needs agreed at the beginning of the cycle and the actions which will be taken to address them.
	Professional development should support achieving objectives and respond to career aspirations.
	Headteacher's annual report to governing body to include teachers' training and development needs and the effectiveness of performance management. (See page 21 for guidance on the content of the report.)

Other issues may be raised and considered at any stage after the planning meeting. If there was a change in the school's circumstances objectives could be re-negotiated.

Classroom observations

Previous position	Revised Regulations
No limit on classroom observation. A minimum of one observation required but this was open-ended and had the potential to lead to excessive monitoring.	Classroom observation limited to no more than three hours per cycle, no requirement to use all of these. *NB this excludes Ofsted observations, local authority observations (using their statutory powers of intervention), and those undertaken for purposes of discharging the statutory duty of evaluating the standards of teaching and learning in the school.* Written feedback given on observation within five days. Must be conducted by a qualified teacher.
Often separate systems of observation operating to inform performance management, the SEF, school improvement planning and other processes.	The school's Performance Management Policy should link to arrangements for school improvement, school self-evaluation and school development planning.
No requirement to have a protocol for classroom observation.	Headteacher must establish a Performance Management Policy which includes a protocol for classroom observation, on which they consult with teachers, and which they seek to agree with trade unions.
No restrictions on other evidence and who can supply it.	Only persons with direct professional knowledge of the work of the teacher/headteacher/support staff member can provide evidence.

Monitoring and support

Previous position	Revised Regulations
No regulations requiring information to be shared or concerns to be raised during the cycle.	There is a regulated process for raising concerns.
No regulations preventing other information not known to the teacher/headteacher from being introduced and considered at the review.	Regulatory provision for raising other concerns or where circumstances change.

The review meeting

Previous position	Revised Regulations
No regulations preventing other information not known to the teacher/headteacher being introduced and considered at the review meeting.	Once the cycle is underway the review of the previous year's objectives will happen in the same meeting as the planning of new objectives. At the review meeting, **review performance against the performance criteria established at the outset**. The outcome of the review meeting will represent the **overall performance** of the teacher/headteacher. In reaching a judgement about the overall performance of the headteacher the governor reviewers could refer to the National Standards for Headteachers. In the case of teachers reference to the Professional Standards for Teachers would be helpful.
No direct link with pay decisions. No clarity on the use of performance management information to inform pay decisions.	The assessment at the review meeting (based on the performance/success criteria) forms the basis for the recommendation for pay progression for the headteacher and eligible teachers. If the reviewee is eligible, the review meeting produces a recommendation on pay progression which must be directed to the governors who make decisions about pay.

The review meeting

Previous position	Revised Regulations
Team leaders can be peers or line managers – peers receive no remuneration for this responsibility.	Reviewer will be the headteacher who may delegate this role in its entirety to the teacher's line manager. Where the headteacher wants to make the decision on pay progression then they need to be the reviewer. The headteacher may review other teachers' planning statements for compliance with the policy and consistency with other statements. This moderation process is not a requirement of headteachers and they may choose not to carry this out where they feel confident that there is no need. The governing body's role in relation to the headteacher's planning statement is one of quality assurance and not moderation. This means that they may choose to nominate the chair or up to three governors to check to ensure that the planning statement is consistent with the school's priorities, and complies with the school's Performance Management Policy and the Regulations. The governing body may review the contents of the plan recorded in the headteacher's statement within 10 days of it being passed to it.
Teachers/headteacher changing schools part way through a cycle or during the two-year period between progression on UPS may have to begin again.	Requirement for schools, if requested by the teacher/headteacher (as the reviewee), to transfer information collected to date if changing schools during a cycle.
Headteacher/teacher/governing body able to take other evidence into account in addition to outcomes of performance management review for pay decisions.	Scope for intervention: headteacher may instruct reviewer to prepare a new statement where headteacher is of the opinion that the statement is inconsistent with statements of other teachers, or does not comply with the Performance Management Policy. (Governing body will carry out this role where headteacher is the reviewee.)

Annex A provides a summary of the process and timings.

Source: TDA training materials (edited)

Policy for support staff

There is no nationally agreed model policy for support staff but Annex B to this book contains a policy produced by Edgbarrow School and Annex C general guidance produced by Banbury School.

Preparing for the planning and review meeting

Identifying and training reviewers

The TDA has produced comprehensive training material for reviewers – headteachers, teachers and governors – and local authorities around the country have been offering it as part of their training programme.

Besides establishing the policy, a number of roles need to be defined within the governing body in order to support the overall performance management cycle. The governing body needs to allocate roles which cover the areas below. It is likely that some governors may have more than one role in the performance management process, such as quality assurance and pay.

Two-three governor reviewers	Optional quality assurance of PM process for HT	Pay committee	Appeals Committee

Source: TDA training materials (edited)

No member of staff can take part in the performance management of the headteacher.

A governing body that is operating strategically will have ensured that the governors involved in the process have undertaken the training provided by the local authority and are able to play their part, whether that is setting and reviewing objectives, deciding pay awards or dealing with appeals.

Some governing bodies take a very structured approach to succession planning, encouraging someone new to the process each year to observe the planning and review meeting in preparation for succeeding one of the more experienced governors the following year.

Effective governing bodies will also ensure that all those members of staff who are acting as reviewers are confident and competent to carry out the role.

The descriptions overleaf match managers who are capable of leading, managing and developing people effectively. They may help to inform the choice of reviewers.

Knowledge	<ul><li>Has in-depth knowledge of professional/subject specialism</li><li>Aware of and committed to achieving the school's vision</li><li>Knows when to make decisions, consult with others, or defer to others for advice</li><li>Aware of the local and national vision for education and curriculum requirements</li><li>Aware of the resources available to support professional development both within and beyond the school</li></ul>
Skill	<ul><li>Confident in analysing evidence including statistical data</li><li>A highly effective (classroom) practitioner</li><li>Able to communicate clearly and concisely</li><li>Well-developed interpersonal, organisational and time-management skills</li><li>Assertive whilst remaining empathetic to reviewee needs</li><li>Able to listen and respond to reviewee's views and concerns</li><li>Able to coach and mentor to develop individuals' and teams' strengths</li><li>Able to solve problems using own initiative and creativity</li><li>Able to support and inspire team</li><li>Able to objectively critique own, individuals' and teams' performance</li><li>Organised and able to delegate as appropriate</li></ul>
Attributes	<ul><li>Adopts high standards of behaviour in their professional role</li><li>Open, approachable and honest</li><li>Committed to distributed leadership, collaboration and co-operative working</li><li>Empathetic whilst maintaining authority</li><li>Gives recognition and values all contributions</li><li>Ensures a safe environment</li><li>A reflective practitioner who is committed to fostering a culture for continuous improvement</li></ul>

Source: based on a proforma produced by Collingwood College and the Professional Standards for Teachers

Self-review

The premise that schools know themselves best underpins the strategy for self-evaluation and the SEF. The same applies to individuals. To stimulate ownership of the performance management process reviewees should be encouraged to reflect on their performance prior to the planning and review meeting. However, that is not compulsory.

Some model proformas to support self-review are included in the section on preparing for the planning and review meeting.

Similarly, to ensure that the meeting is productive reviewers should prepare carefully, ensuring clarity about the:

- reviewee's role
- previous objectives where appropriate
- the school's priorities
- relevant data
- professional standards
- professional development opportunities.

The planning and review meeting

In the case of an established headteacher or member of staff the review of the previous year's performance would precede the setting of new objectives. For a new member of staff or headteacher the meeting would simply address objective-setting. Assuming that the cycle is underway, the meeting would first focus on the review of the previous year's objectives. Reviewers should be able to draw upon:

• evidence gathered in monitoring throughout the year

• the self-review by the reviewee

• input from other colleagues if agreed

• their own preparation notes.

See the following proformas:

PM 1	Self-review for headteachers
PM 2	Self-review for teachers
PM 3	Self-review for support staff
PM 4	Preparation by governor reviewers
PM 5	Preparation by reviewers of teaching staff
PM 6	Preparation by reviewers of support staff
PM 7	Headteacher's review statement
PM 8	Teacher's review statement
PM 9	Support staff member's review statement
PM 10	Headteacher's performance management plan
PM 11	Teacher's performance management plan
PM 12	Support staff member's performance management plan

The guidance says that the planning meeting must consider and determine:

• the reviewee's objectives

• arrangements for observing the reviewee's performance in the classroom (headteachers do not have to be observed teaching)

• any other evidence to be taken into account in assessing performance

• the performance criteria for the above

• support to be provided to the reviewee

• timescales for achievement of the objectives and within which support will be provided

• the reviewee's training and development needs and actions to be taken to address them.

It must have regard to:

• the reviewee's job description

• any relevant pay progression criteria

• any relevant whole-school or team objectives specified in the school improvement plan

• the reviewee's professional aspirations

• the relevant professional standards

- the reviewee's need for a satisfactory work-life balance. The TDA, quoting the National Agreement, defines work-life balance as being about "helping teachers combine work with their personal interests outside of work" and cites working hours and workload as key, but not exclusive, elements of this.

It must:

- be a well-planned event
- in the case of the headteacher, involve the SIP in the planning and in the meeting itself
- be a professional dialogue with all parties playing an active part
- decide specific priorities and actions
- ensure that the number and scope of objectives agreed is realistic and manageable. Remember that the aim is not to set objectives for everything that the reviewee is responsible for, but to focus on three or four elements to gain a clear idea of how s/he approaches their job as a whole.

Objective-setting

The point has already been made that the school improvement plan and the reviewee's job description should underpin the process of setting objectives. Objectives should also be informed by the need to secure work-life balance, recognition of the reviewee's professional aspirations, and reference to the relevant professional standards. There is no specified number or type.

Another important principle here is "measure what you value". When setting objectives it is crucial to make them:

Specific

Measurable

Achievable and Challenging

Relevant

Time limited.

Some things are a lot easier to measure than others – for example, attendance, progress of learners, exclusions. With the less tangible aspects of performance, performance criteria can help to make goals specific. It may be helpful to ask "What will learners/parents/curriculum leaders, etc., be doing that they're not doing now? What will the reviewee do to make that happen?" In addition, surveys can be used to quantify satisfaction levels and to compare and contrast them year on year.

The following examples from Westminster's training materials can be used to stimulate discussion:

- *"To draft a new behaviour policy by December 200X which, after consultation with staff, is agreed by the governing body."*

This objective describes a task or action, not an objective.

It would be better included as an action related to an objective about improving behaviour of specified children, possibly at specified times of the school day. Performance criteria could include a quantified reduction in the number of exclusions and or referrals, fewer complaints from neighbours and a revised policy established by the governing body by a certain date.

- *"The headteacher will take steps to ensure that mathematics is effectively taught in each class and will monitor the teaching, so that Level 3 results match those of similar schools."*

This mixes the objectives with tasks. Also it lacks clear performance criteria, as next year's results for similar schools are not yet known.

This would be better written as:

To ensure *x*% of children achieve L3 in maths in the KS1 SATs in summer 200X.

Performance criteria could include positive contextual value added. Trends over time would also be a relevant factor, as would relative performance of different groups of pupils and pupils' performance across core subjects.

Similarly to write:

- "to improve attainment in maths in KS3"

- "to improve parental involvement"

- "to raise attainment in maths by 5%"

- "to start a lunchtime computer club"

would not give the reviewee a clear indication of what was expected, of what the ultimate goal is. In the third point it would be much clearer to state the current percentage and the desired one.

Some examples of objectives are set out in the individual plans in "The Planning and Review Meeting".

Reviewing performance

The emphasis on performance criteria and the arrangements for gathering additional evidence should facilitate the process of reviewing performance. So too should self-review by the reviewee and careful preparation by the reviewer.

In the discussion itself the reviewer(s) will need to:

- create a supportive environment

- set a constructive tone

- encourage a dialogue

- use active listening

- use open, probing and reflective questions

- analyse and summarise

- make effective reference to evidence

- recognise and praise effort as well as success

- show moral courage when tough messages are necessary

- convert mistakes into learning

- suggest ideas and explore options, guiding reviewees into generating solutions

- know when to move the discussion forward

- make good use of time.

When considering learner progress objectives useful questions are:

- What percentage met their targets?

- What percentage exceeded their targets and why?

- What percentage failed to meet their targets and why?

For each objective there should be a clear recognition of whether the objective was fully met, partly met or not met. The extent to which the performance criteria were met will support the process of making a judgement about each objective. There should be clarity about any issues that might have impeded the reviewee's performance.

Consideration of **overall performance** requires a broader perspective than simply reviewing objectives. For this part of the process reference to the relevant professional standards is useful. For headteachers the key areas of headship are:

- shaping the future
- leading learning and teaching
- developing self and working with others
- managing the organisation
- securing accountability
- strengthening community.

For teachers the aspects covered are:

- professional attributes
- professional knowledge and understanding
- professional skills.

For support staff you could consider performance against:

- professional knowledge and understanding
- professional attributes
- leadership and management (where applicable)
- professional skills
- wider professional effectiveness.

After completing this stage it should be possible to write a summative statement that precedes the decision about whether or not to recommend pay progression.

In making judgements about whether pay progression is merited the following criteria may be helpful.

Summative statements

Excellent performance

- Fulfils all responsibilities of job description to a high standard and achieves a consistently very good or better standard of performance.
- Sets and achieves very challenging objectives.
- Makes a major contribution to the aims and policies of the school, regularly exceeding the requirements of the job description.
- Aspects of work merit dissemination to share good practice.

Performance above expectation

- Fulfils all responsibilities of the post and achieves a consistently good or better standard of performance.
- Sets challenging objectives and achieves the majority of them.
- Sometimes exceeds the requirements of the job description.
- Has many more strengths than areas needing development.

Performance as expected

- Fulfils responsibilities of the post but with scope to extend contribution.

- Achieves consistently satisfactory or better standard of performance.

- Achieves majority of objectives.

- Has strengths but also some areas for development.

Performance below expectations

- Not yet fulfilling all requirements of the job description despite length of tenure.

- Standard of performance is at best satisfactory with some unsatisfactory tasks undertaken.

- Achieves only some objectives.

- Has significant areas for development.

Source: Collingwood College (edited)

Pay progression

The school's pay policy determines the process for considering recommendations for pay progression. A model policy can be found on www.governornet.co.uk. There was a suggestion that RIG and the TDA might produce a more up-to-date version but that has not materialised at the time of writing.

The guidance states that the headteacher must pass on, unchanged, the recommendations made by the reviewers. Governor reviewers pass their recommendations on the headteacher to the relevant committee.

Appeals

The guidance stipulates that any appeal should be deferred until after the moderation process is complete in those cases where the headteacher/governing body has indicated an intention to moderate/quality assure the statements. It points out that governing bodies are required by law to establish procedures for dealing with any grievance teachers may have at work, and these should be used by any reviewee wishing to appeal against any entry on their planning and review statement, including any changes made during the cycle.

For an appeal about pay progression the governors responsible for making decisions about pay would clearly need to delay their decision until any appeal process was completed.

Further guidance on pay is promised from RIG and the TDA and will be available on www.teachernet.gov.uk.

Plotting pay progression

The table overleaf may be helpful in plotting pay progression.

Pay progression information (to be updated at each review) 200X-200X

Reviewee name: _____   Reviewer name: _____

Unqualified

✔	Year
1 ☐	
2 ☐	
3 ☐	
4 ☐	
5 ☐	
6 ☐	
7 ☐	
8 ☐	
9 ☐	
10 ☐	

Newly Qualified

✔	Year
NQT ☐	

Main Professional Scale

✔	Year
MPS1 ☐	
2 ☐	
3 ☐	
4 ☐	
5 ☐	
6 ☐	
THRESHOLD	

Upper Pay Spine

✔		Year
UPS1 **	Year 1	20___
	Year 2	20___
UPS2	Year 1	20___
	Year 2	20___
UPS3	Year 1	20___
	Year 2	20___

** You must serve 2 years on each UPS scale before being eligible for the next level (see below)

Other

✔	Pay range	Year	Point on range
Excellent Teacher ☐			
Advanced Skills Teacher ☐			
Leadership Spine ☐			

Reviewers make pay progression recommendations at the following points only: Upper Pay Spine (UPS)1 – 2 and UPS2 – 3 and for all staff on AST and Leadership spines.

The only exception to this is where the reviewer, in accordance with the school's pay policy, is considering a discretionary additional point provided for in the *School Teachers' Pay and Conditions Document*.

Main professional scale – Once on this scale you should be working towards threshold standards and gathering evidence.

Movement from MPS6 to threshold is by application to the headteacher, using the standard national threshold application form. Applications must be in to the headteacher by the end of November in the year you are eligible to apply.

Upper Pay Spine – Once you have successfully crossed the threshold you go onto the upper pay spine at UPS1. You must be on each UPS level for two years before you are eligible to move up to the next level. You must also have had two successful and consecutive performance management reviews and must not have had a lesson that was judged inadequate after an observation within the last 12 months. You must also be making a "sustained and substantial" contribution to the school and be involved in coaching/mentoring of other colleagues, e.g. ITT/NQT/in-faculty support. Your reviewer is the one who recommends you for pay progression at these points.

Excellent Teacher status – eligible to apply if you have been on UPS3 for a minimum of two years and meet the nationally set criteria and rigorous assessment process.

Advanced Skills Teacher – can apply at any stage. Nationally set criteria and rigorous assessment process.

You cannot retain TLRs if you are an AST.

Source: Banbury School

Monitoring and supporting

The purpose of monitoring is to review whether plans are being implemented and to gather evidence to inform judgements about impact. It creates opportunities to:

- celebrate good progress

- revise objectives if circumstances require it

- provide additional support if the reviewee is struggling to make progress.

There are two key aspects to monitoring – monitoring progress with the objectives and, for teachers, lesson observations. A maximum of three hours of lesson observation per year is stipulated in the guidance. Monitoring progress with objectives will be greatly facilitated if clear performance criteria are agreed at the planning meeting and there is agreement about how and when evidence of progress will be gathered. This can happen throughout the cycle and certainly shouldn't be left till the end, because by then it is too late to take any remedial action.

The model policy includes guidance on establishing a classroom observation policy, and is included here as an example of how one school has interpreted that.

See the following proforma:

PM 13   Classroom observation protocol

PM 14   Lesson observation form 1

PM 15   Lesson observation form 2

PM 16   Lesson observation form 3

PM 17   Interim monitoring form for headteachers and governor reviewers

PM 18   Interim monitoring form for teachers

PM 19   Interim monitoring form for support staff

Evaluating the impact of the policy

One of the key ways in which the governing body evaluates the overall impact of the policy is using the information provided in the headteacher's annual report on implementation. The following is a list of possible contents of that report.

The headteacher's annual report on performance management

The headteacher is required to report annually on the performance management process. The following points could usefully be addressed:

- the allocation of staff to reviewees (structure chart)

- the training provided for reviewers and reviewees

- the percentage of planning meetings that took place on schedule. If less than 100%, what got in the way and what steps have been taken to ensure it doesn't happen again?

- the training needs identified (broad themes) and how they are being addressed

- what impact, if any, is noted at this stage as an outcome of the training

- number of lesson observations that took place and the percentages judged to be unsatisfactory, satisfactory, good, outstanding

- summary of strengths and areas for development identified in lesson observations

- how good practice is being disseminated

- how areas for development are being tackled

- percentage of objectives met, not met, exceeded

- where they weren't achieved, what were the key obstacles to success and how are they being addressed?

Equal opportunities

To ensure that the process is fair and non-discriminatory headteachers should report on race, sex, sexual orientation, disability, religion and belief, age, part-time contracts, trade union membership. The TDA advises that this should be done without identifying individuals or compromising confidentiality.

The headteacher should also report on whether there have been any appeals on the grounds of alleged discrimination under any of those categories.

One of the TDA information sheets is entitled *How to Address Issues of Equality, Fairness and Diversity in the Implementation of Performance Management*. It provides clear and constructive guidance.

The staff perspective on the process

One of the key purposes of the performance management process is to motivate and inspire staff by:

- enabling them to see how their work contributes to achieving the school's key aims

- recognising and celebrating effort as well as success

- ensuring they access appropriate development opportunities

- providing support if they are experiencing difficulty in meeting their objectives.

In view of this it is important that the headteacher's report to the governing body includes feedback from them. The questionnaire opposite may be helpful.

Resources

- *Getting the Best out of Performance Management in Your School*, F. Hartle, K. Everall and C. Baker, Taylor and Francis Books, 2001

- *Helping You Develop: Guidance on Producing a Professional Development Record,* DCSF (ref. DfES 0649/2001), tel. 0845 6022260

- *Professional Standards for Teachers,* TDA, tel. 0845 6060323

- *Performance Management: Support Guide for Governors and Headteachers,* DfES, 2003

- Training and Development Agency, http://www.tda.gov.uk/teachers/performance_management.aspx. This site includes training materials, "how to" sheets and frequently asked questions.

- *The National Standards for Headteachers*, DCSF (ref. DfES/0083/2004), tel. 0845 6022260

Staff perspectives on performance management

Rate the current process 1-4.   1= Strongly disagree   2 = Disagree   3 = Agree   4 = Strongly agree

		Score			
Attitudes		**1**	**2**	**3**	**4**
1	This school has a clear sense of direction and purpose.				
2	The school and my team leader are committed to the performance management process.				
3	I believe it is a valuable experience.				
Skills					
4	My reviewer demonstrates a high level of competence in managing the process.				
5	I am clear about what is expected of me in my job.				
6	My reviewer motivates me to develop and achieve my objectives.				
7	Timely and effective feedback/support is given and received.				
Process					
8	Meetings and observations take place as planned.				
9	The school improvement plan provides a clear focus for my objectives.				
10	My reviewer and I agree objectives which are within my power to achieve.				
11	I have access to appropriate training and development opportunities to help me achieve my objectives.				
12	Monitoring progress towards my objectives is a regular activity.				
13	My efforts as well as my successes are recognised and celebrated.				
14	Judgements about my performance are fair and consistent.				
15	The current link between pay and performance is fair.				
16	Overall, the PM process helps to improve my performance and the performance of the school				

Adapted from a questionnaire in Getting the Best out of Performance Management in Your School, *F. Hartle, K. Everall, and C. Baker*

Preparing for the Planning and Review Meeting

PM 1   **Self-review for headteachers**

PM 2   **Self-review for teachers**

PM 3   **Self-review for support staff**

PM 4   **Preparation by governor reviewers**

PM 5   **Preparation by reviewers of teaching staff**

PM 6   **Preparation by reviewers of support staff**

PM1. Self-review for headteachers

Headteacher review of performance objectives for 200X-200X

Name:
Date of meeting:
Governor reviewers:
1. ....
2. ....
3. ....

Review of progress

Objective 1.
Self-evaluation of progress towards objective and/or additional information e.g. feedback from LA or Ofsted

Objective 2.
Self-evaluation of progress towards objective and/or additional information e.g. feedback from LA or Ofsted

Objective 3.
Self-evaluation of progress towards objective and/or additional information, e.g. feedback from LA or Ofsted

PM1. Self-review for headteachers (2)

Overall performance
Any additional information to contribute to review of overall performance. You might wish to consider the six Key Areas of Headship described in the National Standards for Headteachers: shaping the future; leading learning and teaching; developing self and working with others; managing the organisation; securing accountability; and strengthening community.

Future objectives
In the light of the school's priorities and your own professional aspirations what might constitute an appropriate focus for objectives in the next cycle?

How do you see your career developing and what opportunities might support you in this?

Signature of headteacher _____ Date _____

Ensure that copies of all documentation/evidence to be considered at the review meeting are sent to the reviewers and SIP prior to the meeting.

PM2. Self-review for teachers

Optional

Teacher review of performance objectives for 200X-200X

Name:	
Role:	
Date of meeting:	

---

1. What progress did you make against last year's objectives? What evidence do you have?

2. What other responsibilities outlined in your job description have gone particularly well?

3. Identify any issues that affected your performance last year, either positively or negatively.

4. How effective has any planned support/training/professional development identified at your last meeting been? What have you done as a result of it?

PM2. Self-review for teachers (2)

5. Self-review against Professional Standards for Teachers Provide evidence where possible.	Strengths	Areas for Improvement *(linked to Professional Standards)*
Professional attributes relationships with children and young people, frameworks, communicating and working with others, personal professional development		
Professional knowledge and understanding of teaching and learning, assessment and monitoring, subjects and curriculum, literacy, numeracy and ICT, achievement and diversity, health and well-being		
Professional skills planning, teaching, assessing, monitoring and giving feedback, reviewing teaching and learning, learning environment, teamworking and collaboration		

6. In the light of your answers to the previous questions, and taking into account departmental/ faculty/year team/Key Stage/whole-school priorities, and your own professional aspirations, what would you like to achieve over the next performance management cycle?

7. Outline any support/professional development that would help you to achieve progress in the areas you have identified in questions 5 and 6 above.

8. How do you see your career developing and what opportunities might support you in this?

Ensure that copies of all documentation/evidence to be considered at the review meeting are sent to the reviewer prior to the meeting.

Informed by Banbury School and the Professional Standards for Teachers.

PM3. Self-review for support staff

Optional

Support staff self-review of performance objectives for 200X-200X

Name:
Role:
Date of meeting:
Reviewer:

Previous targets/objectives

What progress have you made with last year's objectives? What evidence do you have?

Before completing this next section you might find it helpful to consider the descriptions overleaf, your job description and the priorities in the school improvement plan.

Draft objectives

In the light of your job description, your self-review and your knowledge of the school's priorities, what would you like to achieve during the next performance management cycle?

PM3. Self-review for support staff (2)

Self-review against professional effectiveness criteria Provide evidence where possible.	Strengths	Areas for Improvement
Professional knowledge and, understanding e.g. of whole-school priorities, standards relevant to role		
Professional attributes e.g. initiative, creativity, efficiency, effort, work rate, accuracy, relationships, communication, commitment, reliability		
Leadership and management (where applicable)		
Professional skills e.g. communication, time-keeping, problem-solving, teamworking		
Wider professional effectiveness e.g. contributions over and above the job description		

Ensure that copies of all documentation/evidence to be considered at the review meeting are sent to the reviewer prior to the meeting.

Source: Collingwood College (edited)

PM4. Preparation by governor reviewers

Name of headteacher:
Date of meeting:
Governor reviewers: 1. ....   2. ....   3. ....

Previous year's objectives
1. If the headteacher has decided to undertake self-review, how and when will that evidence be considered?
2. What in-year monitoring of objectives are we able to draw upon to inform the process?
3. What role have we agreed for the SIP?
4. In the light of the school's priorities and the six Key Areas of Headship described in the National Standards for Headteachers, what might it be appropriate to focus next year's objectives on? (The Key Areas are: shaping the future; leading learning and teaching; developing self and working with others; managing the organisation; securing accountability and strengthening community.)
5. Have all the reviewers and the SIP got copies of the: • the headteacher's self-review   • the school development plan   • the SEF   • the National Standards for Headteachers   • relevant performance management data?

Ensure that copies of all documentation/evidence to be considered at the review meeting are sent to the headteacher and SIP prior to the meeting.

PM5. Preparation by reviewers of teaching staff

Name of reviewee:
Role:
Name of reviewer:

Date of meeting:

Note that where the reviewer is not the director of faculty or head of department it will be necessary to complete this form with them. (Applies if the line manager is not the reviewer.)

1.What progress did the reviewee make against last year's objectives? What evidence do you have?
2. What other responsibilities outlined in her/his job description have gone particularly well?
3. Identify any issues that affected their performance last year, either positively or negatively.
4. How effective has any planned support/training/professional development identified at the last meeting been? What has s/he done as a result of it?

PM5. Preparation by reviewers of teaching staff (2)

5. Review against Professional Standards for Teachers Provide evidence where possible.	Strengths	Areas for Improvement
Professional attributes relationships with children and young people, frameworks, communicating and working with others, personal professional development		
Professional knowledge and understanding of teaching and learning, assessment and monitoring, subjects and curriculum, literacy, numeracy and ICT, achievement and diversity, health and well-being		
Professional skills planning, teaching, assessing, monitoring and giving feedback, reviewing teaching and learning, learning environment, teamworking and collaboration.		

6. In the light of your answers to the previous questions, and taking into account departmental/ faculty/year team/Key Stage/whole-school priorities, what would it be appropriate for the reviewee to try to achieve over the next PM cycle?

7. What support/professional development would help her/him to achieve progress in the areas identified in questions 5 and 6?

8. How do you see her/his career developing and what opportunities might support this?

Ensure that copies of all documentation/evidence to be presented at the review meeting have been sent to the reviewee prior to the meeting.

Informed by Banbury School and the Professional Standards for Teachers

PM6. Preparation by reviewers of support staff

The following form could be used by the reviewer (and other colleagues with an overview of the reviewee's responsibilities if this was agreed with the reviewee at the planning stage).

Name of reviewee:
Role:
Name of reviewer:
Date of meeting:

Previous objectives
What were the objectives and what progress was made with last year's objectives? What evidence do you have?

Before completing the next section consider the descriptions opposite, the reviewee's job description and the priorities in the school improvement plan.

Draft objectives
What might constitute an appropriate focus for objectives for the next performance management cycle?

What support/training would help him/her to achieve them?

PM6. Preparation by reviewers of support staff (2)

Review against professional effectiveness criteria *Provide evidence where possible*	Strengths	Areas for Improvement
Professional knowledge and understanding e.g. of whole-school priorities, standards relevant to role		
Professional attributes e.g. initiative, creativity, efficiency, effort, work rate, accuracy, relationships, communication, commitment, reliability		
Leadership and management (where applicable)		
Professional skills e.g. communication, time-keeping, problem-solving, teamworking.		
Wider professional effectiveness e.g. contributions over and above the job description		

Ensure that copies of all documentation/evidence to be presented at the review meeting have been sent to the reviewee prior to the meeting.

Source: Collingwood College (edited)

The Planning and Review Meeting

PM 7	**Headteacher's review statement**
PM 8	**Teacher's review statement**
PM 9	**Support staff member's review statement**
PM 10	**Headteacher's performance management plan**
PM 11	**Teacher's performance management plan**
PM 12	**Support staff member's performance management plan**

PM7. Headteacher's review statement

Summary of the outcomes in the review of headteacher progress towards objectives in 200X-200X

Note main achievements and state whether each objective was partly met, fully met or not met, citing the evidence underpinning your judgement, and noting any factors that were outside the reviewee's control.

(NB. Prior to 2007 reviewers and headteachers had to agree objectives about pupil progress and leadership and management. This may or may not be the way you decide to continue).

Objective
Objective
Objective

PM7. Headteacher's review statement (2)

Other factors in consideration of overall performance

Reviewers and reviewee might find it helpful to consider the headteacher's performance in relation to the six Key Areas of Headship from the National Standards for Headteachers. These are:

- shaping the future
- leading learning and teaching
- developing self and working with others
- managing the organisation
- securing accountability
- strengthening community.

Summative statement (see pages 18-19)

Training and development needs 200X – 200X

How were they addressed, what difference did the training /development make?

What needs to be addressed in the new cycle?

Pay progression recommendation

The panel recommends/does not recommend a pay award.

Reviewee's comments (optional)

Signatures of reviewers

Signature of reviewee

PM8. Teacher's review statement

Summary of the outcomes in the review of progress towards objectives in 200X-200X

Name of reviewee: _____

Note main achievements and state whether each objective was partly met, fully met or not met, citing the evidence underpinning your judgement and noting any factors that were outside of the reviewee's control.

Objective

Objective

Objective

PM8. Teacher's review statement (2)

Other factors in consideration of overall performance

Reviewer and reviewee might find it helpful to consider the teacher's performance in relation to the Professional Standards for Teachers. These cover:

- professional attributes
- professional knowledge and understanding
- professional skills.

Summative statement (see pages 18-19)

Training and development needs 200X – 200X

How were they addressed, what difference did the training /development make?

What needs to be addressed in the new cycle?

Pay progression recommendation (for eligible teachers)

The reviewer recommends/does not recommend a pay award.

Reviewee's comments (optional)

Signature of reviewee   **Signature of reviewer**

PM9. Support staff member's review statement

Name of reviewee:	
Current job role:	
Review carried out by:	
Date review completed:	
Date of last review:	

Persons consulted: This must include the HoD, HoY (if appropriate), SLT Line Manager. For line managers consultation must include members of team/department.

To what extent have the reviewee's objectives been met? Make a judgement as to whether they were fully met, partly met or not met, citing the evidence base and noting any factors outside reviewee's control.

Objective	Comments
1.	
2.	
3.	

Training and development needs 200X – 200X

How were they addressed, what difference did the training /development make? What needs to be addressed in the new cycle?

Reviewee's comments (optional)

This review has been agreed by (signatures):

Reviewer: _____ Date: _____

Reviewee: _____ Date: _____

Date of next review: _____

PM10. Headteacher's performance management plan

Name:
Date of meeting:
Governor reviewers:
1. _____ 2. _____ 3. _____

Are there any changes to the headteacher's role since the last review? Are any changes to the job description necessary?

Objectives

These must be linked to priorities in the strategic plan and should be such that, if they are achieved, they will contribute to improving the progress of learners. (The example below shows how this might be applied.)

Sample objective To ensure that school meets the requirement to provide access to the core extended services by April 2010

Performance criteria	Actions and interim milestones	Sources of evidence of activities and outcomes	Governing body structures that might provide information
• What will be in place if this objective is achieved? - all key stakeholders consulted - a clear indication, in the school improvement plan, of how different elements of the core offer will help to achieve the school's priorities. For example, improving performance in maths may involve booster classes after school, parent workshops and mentors for learners. Supporting children with mental health issues would involve a range of contacts with, and interventions by, other agencies. - a costed plan in place to ensure sustainability.	• What will the headteacher do and when to progress this objective? This may involve appointing an extended services co-ordinator, depending on the size of the school. If so the headteacher would need to ensure effective line management of that person. It will involve liaison with the LA, other schools and agencies, and consideration of the evidence gathered in the audit of needs and provision. The governing body would need to be involved in decision-making about priorities and the content of the school improvement plan. It may be appropriate to enhance the membership of the governing body to ensure appropriate involvement in decision-making.	• What evidence could be generated in the headteacher's day-to-day work on this objective? - minutes of meetings - progress reports from head/co-coordinator - the school improvement plan - feedback from parents and learners, other schools and agencies - learner progress, behaviour and attainment data.	• Will information arise in the headteacher's/co-ordinator's reports to the GB and committees? • When will the reviewers meet to discuss specific evidence of progress? • Will structured visits by governors generate evidence?

Adapted from Performance Management: Support Guide for Governors and Headteachers, *DfES, 2003*

PM10. Headteacher's performance management plan (2)

Other evidence

What/who?	When and where?	Questions to ask

Support that will be provided for reviewee

If you are happy for the reviewers to keep a copy of this plan please tick the box ❑

Career development aspirations and training needs analysis

Copy this section of the statement to the member of staff with responsibility for continuing professional development.

Individual review of:
Current job role:
Review carried out by:
Date review completed:

What training would further develop the reviewee's professional competence and career plans?
This could include: accessing external training provided by the National College for School Leadership, the TDA, Ofsted or other bodies; visiting other schools; mentoring or being mentored by a peer. It could involve acting as an interim headteacher to support a school in crisis.
Reviewers may also need to be prepared for the situation where the headteacher is preparing for retirement.

PM11. Teacher's performance management plan

Name:	
Date of meeting:	
Reviewer:	

Are there any changes to the reviewee's role since the last review? Are any changes to the job description necessary?

Objectives

These might be whole-school, team or individual but they should be such that, if they are achieved, they will contribute to improving the progress of learners. See below for a sample objective.

Sample objective To ensure that every child achieves or exceeds predicted grades in maths, English and science in the KS2 SATs in summer 200X

Performance criteria	Actions and interim milestones	Sources of evidence of activities and outcomes	Structures that might provide information
• What will be in place if this objective is achieved? - *ongoing collection and analysis of progress data* - *active engagement of parents in their children's learning* - *pupils and parents positive about their experiences* - *differentiated planning* - *effective use of TAs to support specific children* - *consistent implementation of homework policy* - *predicted grades met or exceeded*	• What will the reviewee do and when to progress this objective? - *work closely with TA to identify potential under-achievers* - *put in place personalised intervention strategies* - *inform/liaise with parents, providing guidance on how they can support*	• What evidence will be generated in day-to-day work on this objective? - *pupil tracking data* - *lesson plans* - *children's work* - *feedback from parents (homework diaries)* - *SATs results*	• Will information be generated in school self-evaluation activities? • When will the reviewer and reviewee meet to discuss specific evidence of progress?

Repeat for subsequent objectives.

Adapted from Performance Management: Support Guide for Governors and Headteachers, *DfES, 2003*

PM11. Teacher's performance management plan (2)

Observations

Lesson to be observed	Date	Place	Focus of observation	Observer Note if this will be the reviewer or another colleague such as headteacher or Head of Department

Other evidence

What/who?	When and where?	Questions to ask

Support that will be provided for reviewee

Reviewer to keep a copy.

Career development aspirations and training needs analysis

Copy this section of the statement to the member of staff with responsibility for continuing professional development.

Individual review of:
Current job role:
Review carried out by:
Date review completed:

What training would further develop the reviewee's professional competence and career plans?

1. Observation of another colleague	2. Visit to another school	3. Internal training
4. External training	5. Buddying/mentoring	6. Job-shadowing
7. Private reading/research	8. Action research	9. Job rotation
Recommendations		

PM12. Support staff member's performance management plan

Name:
Date of meeting:
Reviewer:

Objectives

These might be whole-school, team or individual but they should be such that, if they are achieved, they will contribute to improving the progress of learners. A sample objective is given below.

Sample objective To ensure that the first performance management cycle for administrative staff is completed by October 200X.

Performance criteria	Actions and interim milestones	Sources of evidence of activities and outcomes	Structures that might provide information
• What will be in place if this objective is achieved? - *policy in place for support staff that has been agreed by staff, unions and the governing body* - *reviewers identified and trained* - *all relevant staff briefed on the process* - *initial meetings, interim monitoring and review meetings happen on schedule* - *CPD strategy influenced by outcomes from initial meetings* - *positive feedback from administrative staff*	• What will the reviewee do and when to progress this objective? - *consultation with all relevant staff and unions by* .... - *present policy to governing body on* .... - *use external consultant to train reviewers and reviewees by* .... - *organise schedule for initial planning meetings to take place by* .... - *ensure that all individual plans are agreed and filed securely by* .... - *check at regular intervals that reviewers are monitoring progress* - *report to headteacher on first year of implementation by 1 Dec 200X*	• What evidence will be generated in day-to-day work on this objective? - *minutes of consultation meetings* - *drafts of the policy* - *paperwork from the training sessions including feedback from participants* - *individual plans* - *CPD strategy* - *interim monitoring records*	• Will information be generated in school self-evaluation activities? • When will the reviewer and reviewee meet to discuss specific evidence of progress?

Repeat for subsequent objectives.

Adapted from Performance Management: Support Guide for Governors and Headteachers, *DfES, 2003.*

PM12. Support staff member's performance management plan (2)

Observations

Activity to be observed	Date	Place	Focus of observation	**Observer** Note if this will be the reviewer or another colleague such as headteacher or Head of Department

Other evidence

What/who?	When and where?	Questions to ask

Support that will be provided for reviewee

Reviewer to keep a copy.

Training needs

Copy this section of the statement to the member of staff with responsibility for continuing professional development.

Individual review of:
Current job role:
Review carried out by:
Date review completed:

What training would further develop the reviewee's professional competence and career plans?

1. Observation of another colleague	2. Visit to another school	3. Internal training
4. External training	5. Buddying/mentoring	6. Job-shadowing
7. Private reading/research	8. Action research	9. Job rotation
Recommendations		

Informed by Banbury School

Monitoring and Support

PM 13 **Classroom observation protocol**

PM 14 **Lesson observation form 1**

PM 15 **Lesson observation form 2**

PM 16 **Lesson observation form 3**

PM 17 **Interim monitoring form for headteachers and governor reviewers**

PM 18 **Interim monitoring form for teachers**

PM 19 **Interim monitoring form for support staff**

PM13. Classroom observation protocol

The governing body is committed to ensuring that classroom observation is developmental and supportive, and that those involved in the process will:

- carry out the role with professionalism, integrity and courtesy

- evaluate objectively

- report accurately and fairly

- respect the confidentiality of the information gained.

The total period for classroom observation arranged for any teacher will not exceed three hours per cycle, having regard to the individual circumstances of the teacher. There is no requirement to use all of the three hours. The amount of observation for each teacher should reflect and be proportionate to the needs of the individual. In this school "proportionate to need" will be determined by the reviewer.

The arrangements for classroom observation will be included in the plan and will include the amount of observation, specify its primary purpose, any particular aspects of the teacher's performance which will be assessed, the duration of the observation, when during the performance management cycle the observation will take place, and who will conduct the observation.

Where evidence emerges about the reviewee's teaching performance that gives rise to concern during the cycle classroom observations may be arranged in addition to those recorded at the beginning of the cycle, subject to a revision meeting being held in accordance with the Regulations.

Information gathered during the observation will be used, as appropriate, for a variety of purposes, including informing school self-evaluation and school improvement strategies in accordance with the school's commitment to streamlining data collection and minimising bureaucracy and workload burdens on staff.

In keeping with the commitment to supportive and developmental classroom observation those being observed will be notified in advance.

Classroom observations will only be undertaken by persons with QTS.

In addition, classroom observation will only be undertaken by those who have had adequate preparation and have the appropriate professional skills to undertake it and to provide constructive oral and written feedback and support, in the context of professional dialogue between colleagues.

Oral feedback will be given as soon as possible after the observation and no later than the end of the following working day. It will be given during directed time in a suitable, private environment.

Written feedback will be provided within five working days of the observation taking place. If issues emerged from an observation that were not part of the focus of the observation as recorded in the planning and review statement these should also be covered in the written feedback and the appropriate action taken in accordance with the Regulations and guidance.

The written record of feedback also includes the date on which the observation took place, the lesson observed and the length of the observation. The teacher has the right to append written comments on the feedback document. No written notes in addition to the written feedback will be kept. All observations will be recorded on the school's observation sheet.

A headteacher has a duty to evaluate the standards of teaching and learning and to ensure that proper standards of professional performance are established and maintained. Heads have a right to drop in to inform their monitoring of the quality of learning. At this school drop-ins will be undertaken by the headteacher supported by members of the Senior Leadership Team.

Drop-ins will only inform the performance management process where evidence arises which merits the revision of the performance management planning statement, in accordance with the Regulations.

Source: Edgbarrow School

Lesson observation forms

Three different approaches to lesson observations follow. You can use whichever one seems most appropriate to your circumstances. Essentially they focus the reviewer on:

- **evidence** – what the reviewee says and does

- **analysis** – what were the strengths and what aspects could have been better?

- **action** – what needs to happen to bring about improvement?

All three call for a judgement to be made using the Ofsted grading system. The third form makes clear that the same format will be used for a variety of purposes.

PM14. Lesson observation form 1

Teacher:	Subject:	Number of pupils:
Observer:	Year group:	
Date:		

Start of the lesson

	Comment (focus on the learning)
Students welcomed/greeted on entry.	
Class settled; register taken; comment on late pupils; no wasted time.	
Distribution of equipment/books managed effectively.	
Learning objectives and learning outcomes shared clearly/reinforced.	
Recap of work from previous lesson.	
Relevant "starter" activity used, if appropriate.	
Appropriate, well-structured lesson plan communicated to learners.	

Main part of the lesson

	Comment (focus on the learning)
Teacher's explanations are clear.	
Effective use of open questioning.	
Pace is maintained and students are engaged in the tasks.	
Student grouping is managed well, and, where appropriate, effectively engineered.	
Activities are appropriate to the needs of the learners, engaging, varied and accurately pitched.	
Those with additional learning needs have work which is well tailored to their needs.	
Ongoing assessment of learning is evident. Teacher intervenes and monitors progress.	
Teacher refers to students' individual targets or needs. Expectation is high.	
Students are encouraged to take responsibility for own learning. They are able to question/take initiative.	
Evidence of self-assessment and peer-assessment.	
Resources are used to engage and extend learners.	
Students make good progress in knowledge, understanding and skills.	
The teacher's subject knowledge and expertise lends confidence to their teaching styles.	
Students are well behaved. Teacher manages the class effectively.	
Time management is effective.	
Cross-curricular links: Business Enterprise/ ICT.	
Cross-curricular links: Literacy/ Numeracy.	

PM14. Lesson observation form 1 (2)

End of the lesson

	Comment (focus on the learning)
Plenary / review takes place and is linked to original learning objectives.	
Agenda for next lesson is discussed.	
Appropriate, relevant homework set.	
Students dismissed in an orderly manner.	

Strengths of the lesson

Areas for development

Action agreed

Overall judgement:

❑ = 1 Outstanding   ❑ = 2 Good   ❑ = 3 Satisfactory   ❑ = 4 Inadequate

Reviewee's comments

Signed

Reviewer _____

Reviewee _____

Source: Edgbarrow School (edited)

PM15. Lesson observation form 2

Teacher:	Observer:	Date:	Lesson:	Overall Grade:
Subject:	Year:	Grouping:	Number present M/F:	Support Staff:

Checklist of documentation provided:- ✓ / ✗	Brief description of lesson including learning objectives
Lesson plan ❏	
Student attainment data ❏	
SEN profile ❏	
Group IEP ❏	

What went well..........	Even better if ....

Overall evaluation and summary of lesson (summarise here which features had the most effect, either positively or negatively on student's progress)

Any other features that need noting (ie, curriculum time, literacy/numeracy, ICT, inclusion, punctuality, safety, health, enjoyment, contribution to the community, economic well-being)

Action agreed

Teacher comment

Signature _____   Date _____

Signature of reviewer _____

When using the Ofsted criteria on the next page, unless pupil progress descriptor is satisfactory or better, the lesson cannot be judged in its entirety to be satisfactory or better. Tick the relevant box in the form for each aspect of teaching and learning.

Source: Banbury School

Aspect of teaching and learning	Outstanding (1)	Good (2)	Satisfactory (3)	Inadequate (4)
Pupil progress	All learners make very good progress.	Virtually all learners make good progress.	Most learners make the progress that should be expected of them.	Learners generally, or significant groups of them, do not make adequate progress because the teaching is unsatisfactory.
Behaviour and attitudes to learning	All learners are thriving as a result of the teaching; motivated, on task, clearly enjoying their learning.	Virtually all learners are on task, motivated and showing positive attitudes towards their learning.	Most learners are on task, motivated and enjoying their work.	Learners generally, or significant groups of them, do not enjoy their work and their behaviour is often inappropriate.
Quality of classroom relationships	The excellent teacher-pupil relationships modelled in the classroom are especially conducive to learning and personal development.	Good teacher: pupil relationships in the classroom help to develop a secure and friendly environment in which to learn.	Teacher-pupil relationships provide a satisfactory basis for learning and personal development.	The poor relationship between teachers and pupils in the classroom is hindering learning and pupils' personal development.
Teacher's subject knowledge	High levels of subject expertise underpins successful T and L.	Good subject knowledge adds confidence to teaching.	Teacher has a secure knowledge of the curriculum and course requirements.	Teacher's knowledge of the curriculum and course requirements are inadequate.
Meeting learners' needs and the level of challenge	All learners are suitably challenged by the pace and depth of the learning, with work sensitively matched to the needs of individuals.	Virtually all learners are suitably challenged with work closely matched to their different capabilities.	The level of challenge is sufficient for most learners, though some might make more progress with different tasks.	The level of challenge is often wrongly pitched for learners, with work badly matched to learners' starting points.
Teaching methods and use of resources	Methods and use of resources (e.g. ICT) are precisely judged and imaginatively selected to engage and extend all learners.	A good range of teaching methods and carefully chosen resources are used to develop learning effectively.	The use of teaching methods and resources is sufficient to encourage and engage learners.	The teaching methods and resources used do not sufficiently engage and encourage learners.
Assessment for learning	Thorough and forensic assessment (incl. questioning) successfully underpins teaching and all learners have a clear idea of how to improve.	Assessment of learners (incl. use of questioning) is regular, consistent and accurate, informing learners of how to improve.	Assessment (incl. use of questioning) is adequate for teachers to monitor learners' progress and plan their lessons, and most learners know what to do to improve.	Assessment (incl. use of questioning) is not frequent or accurate enough to monitor learners' progress, leaving learners not knowing well enough how to improve.
Developing independent learning skills	Learners are equipped to take full advantage of independent learning opportunities, which are effectively integrated to deliver learning objectives.	The development of independent learning skills and confidence is encouraged through the well-judged setting of learning activities.	Independent learning is adequately developed and utilised in achieving the learning objectives.	Not enough independent learning takes place or is ineffective when used.
Relationships with TAs and /support staff	TAs are effectively integrated in supporting learning.	TAs are well-deployed to support learning.	TA support is adequately utilised but could be more effective in supporting learning.	The support of TAs is inadequately utilised in helping learners to succeed.

PM16. Lesson observation form 3

| Class: | Teacher: | Date: | Time: From: To: |
| | No. of Pupils | No. of Support Staff | Subject: Observer: |

Context: description of lesson purpose, setting and curriculum focus

Commentary on the lesson: emphasising the impact of teaching on learners' attainment and progress

Significant features

Strengths	Development points

Overall lesson quality (circle one)　　**outstanding**　　　　**good**　　　**satisfactory**　　　**inadequate**

Reviewee's comments

Action agreed

Signed

Reviewer _____　　Reviewee _____

PM16. Lesson observation form 3 (2)

Quality of teaching: evaluation criteria

Grade	Characteristics
Outstanding (1)	• Teaching is at least good in all, or nearly all, respects and is exemplary in significant elements. • All pupils thrive and make exceptionally good progress.
Good (2)	• Pupils make good progress and show good attitudes to their work. • Good subject knowledge lends confidence to the teaching style. • Learners are engaged and encouraged to work independently. • Unsatisfactory behaviour is managed effectively. • The level of challenge stretches without inhibiting. • Accurate assessment is used to tailor work to the full range of pupils' learning needs and informs them how to improve their work. • Pupils are guided to assess their work themselves. • Teaching Assistants and other classroom helpers are well-directed to support learning. • Pupils with additional needs have work well matched to their needs based on a good diagnosis of them.
Satisfactory (3)	• Teaching is inadequate in no major respect and may be good in some respects. • Pupils enjoy their education. • Pupils make the progress that should be expected of them.
Inadequate (4)	• Progress is unsatisfactory, either for pupils generally or for particular groups, because teaching is unsatisfactory. • Pupils do not enjoy their work. • Behaviour is often inappropriate and is not adequately managed. • The teacher has inadequate subject knowledge. • The level of challenge is often wrongly pitched. • The methods used do not sufficiently engage and encourage the pupils. • Not enough independent learning takes place. • Assessment is not frequent or accurate enough to monitor pupils' progress. • The teacher does not have a clear understanding of the pupils' learning needs. • Pupils do not know how to improve their work. • Teaching Assistants are inadequately helped to support pupils' learning.

Source: Uxbridge Technology College (edited)

PM17. Interim monitoring form for headteachers and governor reviewers

Date of meeting:
Reviewers:
Headteacher:

Objective	Progress noted citing specific performance criteria	Evidence base This could come from headteacher's reports to the governing body, Ofsted, LA monitoring, direct observation by governors while on visits, and/or reports by members of staff to the governing body and committees.	Comments

Do any objectives need to be revised? If so insert revised objective.

New/revised objective

Performance criteria	Actions and interim milestones	Sources of evidence of activities and outcomes	Structures that might provide information

Adapted from Performance Management: Support Guide for Governors and Headteachers, *DfES, 2003*

Does anything else need to happen for the headteacher to meet any objective set? If so, describe below.

Any CPD required that has not been actioned? **Yes** ❑ **No** ❑   If "Yes" describe and note what needs to be done.

Signatures of reviewers   **Signature of reviewee**

_____   _____   _____   _____

PM18. Interim monitoring form for teachers

Date of meeting:
Reviewers:
Reviewee:

Objective	**Progress noted** citing specific performance criteria	**Evidence base**	**Comments**

Do any objectives need to be revised? (Changes in job description/issues/concerns arising, emergent needs of school) If so insert revised objective.

New/revised objective

Performance criteria	**Actions and interim milestones**	**Sources of evidence of activities and outcomes**	**Structures that might provide information**

Adapted from Performance Management: Support Guide for Governors and Headteachers, *DfES, 2003*

Does anything else need to happen in order for the reviewee to meet any objective set? If so, describe below.

Any CPD required that has not been actioned?   **Yes** ❏   **No** ❏

If "Yes" describe and note what needs to be done.

Signed   Reviewer _____   **Reviewee** _____

PM19. Interim monitoring form for support staff
To be completed by the reviewer and reviewee at the interim monitoring meeting

| Name of reviewee: |
| Name of reviewer: |
| Date: |

1. Are the objectives set at the performance management planning meeting still appropriate?

	Yes	No
Objective 1	❑	❑
Objective 2	❑	❑
Objective 3	❑	❑

If you have ticked "No" to any objective give a brief explanation, e.g. significant changes to job description, issues/concerns arising, emergent needs of school.

Would a revised objective be more appropriate? If so enter details here.

Performance criteria	Actions and interim milestones	Sources of evidence of activities and outcomes	Structures that might provide information

Adapted from Performance Management: Support Guide for Governors and Headteachers, *DfES, 2003*

PM19. Interim monitoring form for support staff (2)

2. Is reasonable progress being made to meet the set objectives by the time of the next performance management cycle in approximately six months' time?

	Yes	No
Objective 1	❏	❏
Objective 2	❏	❏
Objective 3	❏	❏

What evidence have you considered?

If you have ticked "No" to any objective, give a brief explanation.

```



```

3. Does anything else need to happen for the reviewee to meet any objective set? If so, describe below.

```



```

	Yes	No
4. Any CPD required that has not been actioned?	❏	❏

If "Yes" describe and note what needs to be done:

```



```

Signed

Reviewer _____   **Reviewee** _____

Attach a copy of this form to each copy of the individual plan.

Source: Banbury School (edited)

Annexes

Annex A. Process and timings

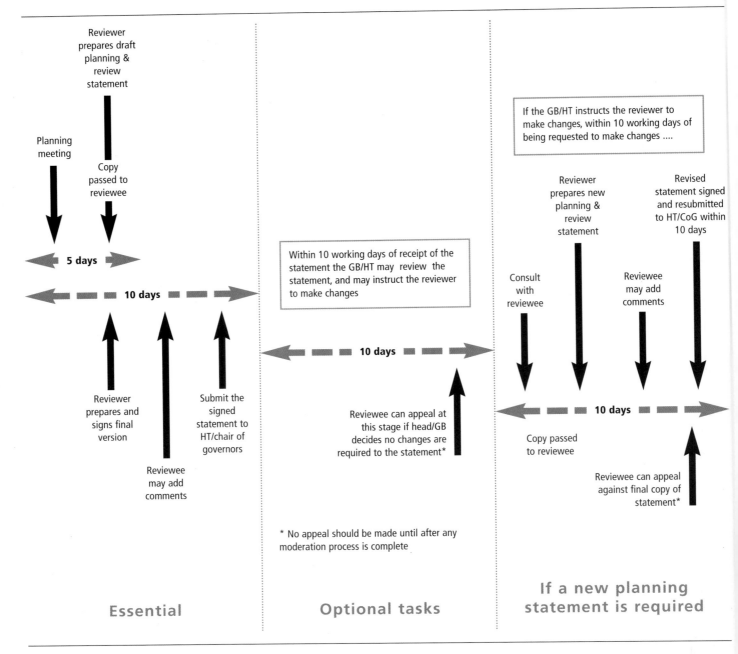

Annex B. Support staff performance management policy

1. Rationale

At Edgbarrow School, governors are committed to performance management. The process is tailored to meet the needs of the school and will assist the school to meet its aims and to deliver the school development plan. Additionally the process is designed to facilitate the development of support staff in gaining access and support to develop their career. The implementation of the performance management arrangements will be on the basis of:

- **Fairness**

  We all need to be aware of the potential for unconscious discrimination and to avoid assumptions about individuals based on stereotypes.

- **Equal opportunity**

  All support staff will be encouraged and supported to achieve their potential through agreeing objectives, undertaking development and having their performance assessed.

This policy covers all support staff who work 20 hours or more per week or support staff who work less than 20 hours per week and have voluntarily chosen to participate in the process.

The school's policy is intended to ensure that the performance of each member of the support staff is reviewed on an annual basis and that an exchange of views will take place between the reviewee and their reviewer.

The benefits of performance management in terms of improved communication and enhanced performance, both for the individual and for the school, will only be achieved by the continuous commitment of all those involved in the process.

The support staff performance management policy has been designed to meet the following specific objectives:

1. to assist staff in performing their roles to the best of their ability and maximise their contribution to the school's overall objectives and targets

2. to identify individual training needs

3. to highlight the potential that each individual has to develop within his/her current position or another role

4. to provide a framework where managers can support their teams.

2. Responsibilities

Performance management is a shared responsibility. The governing body will be involved in agreeing the school's performance management policy for support staff, it will ensure the performance of support staff at the school is regularly reviewed, and it will monitor and evaluate the performance management process. The headteacher is responsible for implementing the school's performance management policy and ensuring that performance management reviews take place.

3. Roles

The **reviewee** is the member of support staff whose performance is being reviewed.

A **reviewer** is a member of staff who leads the performance management review process including meetings and report writing. A reviewer will normally be the reviewee's immediate line manager. Reviewers must have adequate contact with the individuals for whom they are responsible, so that meaningful objectives can be set. Reviewers must undertake training to set objectives and hold performance management reviews.

The reviewee's responsibilities:

- to understand the performance management process
- to understand fully the requirements of their job
- to discuss and agree their objectives with their reviewer
- to receive feedback in a constructive way
- to prepare for the performance review adequately.

The reviewer's responsibilities:

- to ensure he/she understands the performance management review process and has undertaken the required training
- to ensure the process starts at the appropriate time and to complete all the necessary stages throughout the reporting period
- to discuss and agree objectives and training needs with the reviewee
- to support the reviewee in their development
- to monitor the reviewee's performance and provide feedback and coaching as necessary
- to prepare adequately for performance management review interviews.

4. Practices and procedures

A formal system of performance management makes sure that performance review happens regularly, to a set standard and to agreed deadlines. It means that performance review is backed up by sound evidence and based on firm objectives. The performance management process involves a three-stage annual cycle.

Planning

The cycle commences with a discussion between the reviewee and his/her reviewer to review the job description and record the individual's performance objectives for the forthcoming year. At the same time discussion should take place regarding the training and development needs of the reviewee.

New employees joining the school part way through the performance management cycle should aim to complete some initial objectives within three months of commencing employment. Reviewers should ensure that objectives in this instance should be realistically progressed in the remaining time left before the end of the review cycle.

Monitoring

During this phase the reviewer will undertake observations of the reviewee so that they will be in a position to make an informed judgement regarding performance and progress against objectives. Monitoring should take place during the summer term.

Reviewing

This will be a formal meeting between the reviewer and the reviewee to discuss achievements and to identify any development needs. Prior to this meeting the reviewee will have completed and submitted the reviewee's preparation sheet. A written review will be completed by the reviewer to record the main points and the conclusion reached. This statement must be completed within ten working days. The formal review statement will then be given to the reviewee who will have the opportunity to formally comment on the Support Staff Performance Management Review form. Once agreed a copy of the document will be given to the headteacher.

5. Confidentiality and access to outcomes

The review statement is a personal and confidential document and will be kept in a secure place. The principles and provisions of the Data Protection Act 1998 will be followed at all times by those who have access to the documents.

There will only be two copies of the review statement, one held by the job holder and the other by the headteacher in a central file, to which the reviewer or governors responsible for making decisions regarding pay can request access.

The review statements will be held for at least three years.

6. Appeals

Details of the appeals process are covered in the school's pay policy.

Source: Edgbarrow School (edited)

Annex C. General guidance for performance management of support staff

Performance management folders, containing the appropriate paperwork, will be sent out prior to the performance management week. Reviewers will have the blank paperwork for their reviewees, apart from the Self-Review form.

Self-review

The self-review is a crucial part of the performance management process, allowing each individual to take responsibility for their own professional development and review. All staff should complete a Self-Review form in advance of the review meeting. **The completed Self-Review form should then be taken to the review meeting**, where it will form part of the initial discussions.

Reviewer Preparation form

The Reviewer form should be completed by the reviewer prior to the review meeting. This is an important part of the review process and it too will form part of the review meeting discussions.

Teacher review for support staff

The Teacher Review for Support Staff form is the means by which identified members of the teaching staff who work closely with the reviewee can have an input into the review. This is an important additional element to the review process. The teacher will be asked to complete the form in advance of the review meeting and it will form part of the review meeting discussions.

The review meeting

1) Each review meeting should take approximately 1 hour.

2) The reviewee should complete the Self-Review form prior to the review meeting and the reviewer a review meeting reviewer's preparation form. These should be brought to the meeting and will form the basis for discussion.

3) At the start of the review meeting the reviewee needs to review and if necessary revise the job description, in discussion with the reviewer. Main responsibilities and priorities for the coming year need to be recorded. Copies of these will be made to personnel files and team leaders.

4) During this meeting the previous year's objectives will be discussed, and progress against them evaluated, using evidence collected from members of the teaching staff who have been asked for feedback, where relevant. On the basis of this, the reviewer will be required to complete the Performance Review Statement. During the review meeting the outline of statement should be discussed and rough notes made.

5) A copy of the Performance Review Statement must be given to the reviewee by the reviewer within 10 days of the review meeting. The reviewee then has 10 days to add comments to this statement before handing it to the headteacher's PA. This is a confidential document and will be stored in locked personnel files with copies to the headteacher and reviewee.

During the review meeting an individual plan form must be completed. This form records up to three objectives which should be set for the coming year. Objectives should reflect the nature of the reviewee's responsibilities and the priorities in the school development plan. Training and development needs and how they will be addressed should be recorded at the end of the form. That section alone should be copied to the member of staff who has lead responsibility for continuing professional development. However, it is also for the reviewee to be pro-active in identifying any training/courses relevant to the needs recorded on the CPD Action Plan as the year progresses.

6) The individual plan form is a confidential document and copies will be held by the headteacher and the reviewee. The reviewer will have access to the form for the process of ongoing monitoring.

7) At the end of the review process all forms should be handed in to the headteacher's PA. This should be done within 20 days of the review meeting.

Appeals

1) Individual objectives. The reviewer should record the objectives that will apply for the coming year. These should be jointly agreed if possible. If there are any differences of opinion about these the reviewee may add comments to the individual plan.

2) Reviewees can record their dissatisfaction with aspects of the review on the Review Statement. Where these cannot be resolved with the reviewer, they can raise their concerns with the headteacher.

3) Where an appeal is made about the Performance Review Statement, the review officer (the headteacher) is responsible for reviewing the appeal. This should be done within ten days of receiving the appeal. The headteacher may order the Performance Review Statement to stand, may amend the statement, or order that parts of the review or the whole review be repeated. Where a new review or part review is ordered, this should be carried out within 15 working days.

Six-month review

A six-month, intermediate, review will be conducted by the reviewer and reviewee. This is intended to be a short meeting to review the progress relating to the objectives set during the planning meeting and to take any appropriate action, if necessary, to enable the targets to be met.

Checklist for reviewees

Before the review meeting

Have you:

1) received your performance management folder

2) checked who your reviewer is

3) completed your Self-Review form

4) read through your job description noting where changes are needed?

The review meeting

1. Discuss the contents of your self-review with the reviewer. Focus first on your achievements and strengths.

2. Look at your job description together and if necessary revise the job description to ensure that the tasks you carry out are recorded.

3. Discuss evidence that has been gathered by you (optional) and your reviewer. On the basis of this, work through each of the objectives that were agreed last year (where relevant) and discuss the extent to which they've been achieved. Your reviewer will use this discussion to complete the Performance Review Statement. Within ten days of your review meeting your reviewer should give you a final version of your Performance Review Statement. You have a further ten days to add comments to this before handing it to the headteacher's PA.

4. Share your thoughts on areas for development and possible objectives for the coming year. Remember they have to be linked to your job description and the school's priorities.

5. Agree up to three objectives.

6. Ensure all sections on the individual plan are complete and that the continuing professional development action plan section has been completed.

7. Remember that objectives should be agreed by the reviewer and reviewee wherever possible. However, if you are unhappy with the objectives set please add your comments.

8. Once the review meeting has finished ensure that both you and the reviewer have signed all the relevant paperwork. Your reviewer will now pass them on to the headteacher's PA.

Checklist for reviewers

Before the review meeting

Have you:

1) received your performance management folder

2) checked who you are reviewing

3) arranged the time and venue of the review

4) received the completed Self-Review form where relevant

5) completed the Review Meeting Reviewer's form?

The review meeting

The meeting, although a professional discussion, should be led by the reviewer. Ensure that all forms are completed during the meeting and taken to the headteacher's PA, and that the final version of the Performance Review Statement is completed within ten days of the review meeting and handed to the reviewee. The reviewee then has ten days to add comments before s/he hands it in to the headteacher's PA.

1) Discuss the reviewee's self-review, focusing first on their achievements and strengths. Add any positive comments that you noted from your review meeting reviewer's preparation form.

2) Look at the reviewee's job description and ensure that it is up to date, making any amendments on the job description if necessary. Together, work out what the key priorities are for her/him over the coming year.

3) Listen to the reviewee's thoughts on possible areas for development and possible objectives for the coming year. Add any thoughts of your own.

4) Set up to three objectives for the coming year.

5) Ensure that objectives are linked clearly to the reviewee's job description and to the school development plan.

6) Complete the continuing professional development section of the individual plan in consultation with the reviewee. Where possible try to suggest ways to use the vast expertise in the school, e.g. suggest they observe a member of staff who has expertise in an area that the reviewee needs to develop, has a meeting with them to discuss strategies, etc. If you do suggest external training emphasise to the reviewee that it isn't guaranteed.

7) Evidence – decide who the reviewee would like you to speak to and agree the questions they want you to ask. Record this on the Individual Plan. When reviewing a teaching assistant agree on a member of staff who they work closely with, who will then be asked to complete the teaching assistant's monitoring form at the end of the academic year.

8) Ideally the targets you set should be agreed by the reviewer and the reviewee. If agreement isn't reached the reviewer has the right to record what he or she feels is inappropriate and the reviewee can add their own comments to it. If disagreement arises, reflect on your judgements and, if they stand, ensure that the reviewee records his/her views on the plan.

Check that all sections of the individual plan including the continuing professional development action plan are complete and that both you and the reviewee have signed them. Now return these to the headteacher's PA along with the job description.

Source: Banbury School (edited